STORY PAINTER

The Life of Jacob Lawrence

by John Duggleby

chronicle books · san francisco

No. 1 from the *Migration of the Negro* series, 1940–41

Chapter 1

THE GREAT MIGRATION

Young Jacob Lawrence knew the feeling of moving. His family was part of the largest migration of black people since the days of slavery.

In 1910, nine out of ten African-Americans lived in the southern United States, where they had been slaves before the Civil War. But over the next twenty years, after slavery ended, they fled by the millions to cities in the North. Some left because they had heard that there were better jobs in the North. Others wanted to escape the beatings, even killings, that blacks still suffered at the hands of some white southerners. They felt that in the North their families could live in safety and comfort.

> I pick up my life
> And take it away
> On a one-way ticket—
> Gone up North,
> Gone out West,
> Gone!
> — *Langston Hughes*

To those fleeing the South, the North sounded like the "Promised Land" in the Bible. They felt much like the slaves whom Moses led to freedom. Two of those who made the journey North—a woman named Rose from Virginia and a man named Jacob from South Carolina—met and married in Atlantic City, New Jersey. In 1917, they had a son—Jacob Lawrence Jr., or Jake, as most people called him.

Living in the North was more difficult than the Lawrences expected. Even there, they found that many jobs were open only to white people. And the surge of African-Americans migrating to northern cities meant even more competition for what work they could find. By the time Jake was six years old, he had lived in three different cities: Atlantic City, and Easton and Philadelphia, Pennsylvania.

Photo of Jacob as a six-year-old boy with his mother and siblings, 1923

But still, Jake's family saw that things could be worse. As they settled in Philadelphia, they met other southern blacks even poorer than they were. "A new family came up last night with absolutely nothing," Jake's mother would tell his father. "Why don't you dig out a few coals from the furnace? I'll pull together some food and old clothes." Sometimes the new arrivals talked in hushed tones about witnessing a lynching—when a black person was hanged to death from a tree—back home. By comparison, Philadelphia didn't seem so bad.

When Jake was about seven years old, his father drifted away. His mother was left alone to raise the family. Since Jake was the oldest, he was often expected to care for his brother and sister while his mother worked cleaning houses.

While Jake wasn't fond of baby-sitting, he liked the city where he lived. Philadelphia was one of the biggest cities in the North, but it still had a lot of open space. Like most of his neighbors, Jake lived in a small brownstone house. An open lot nearby was his playground. When he wasn't watching his brother and sister, he liked to play by himself, climbing trees and chasing birds.

Jake especially liked to catch insects. He loved the shapes of the ants, grasshoppers, and giant cicadas that scrambled across the lot. Sometimes he drew their forms on scraps of paper.

*The Ant and the
Grasshopper*, 1969

Tombstones, 1942

A day spent exploring and drawing on his own was a real treat for Jake. And if his mother had scrapple waiting for him on the dinner table, it was perfect. Scrapple was made from ground pork mixed with cornmeal, then sliced up and fried in a skillet. It was considered "poor people's food," but it felt very rich in Jake's belly.

Soon, times became harder. When Jake was about ten, his mother gave him some sad news. She couldn't get enough work in Philadelphia. She was moving to New York, which was a bigger city with more jobs. Jake and his brother and sister would have to stay behind in Philadelphia until she was settled. Jake's mother promised to send for them as soon as she could.

But Jake's mother found that work was also scarce in New York. While she struggled to save money, Jake was shuffled in and out of several homes in Philadelphia. He and his brother and sister were separated from one another, as few black families at that time could afford to feed three extra children.

Jake missed his family. He remembered stories he had been told about slaves in the old days. Sometimes a family was split forever when parents and children were sold to different people. "Is this really any different?" Jake wondered.

This Is Harlem, 1942

Chapter 2

THE PROMISED LAND

After three long years, Jake's mother finally had enough money to move her children to New York. "Welcome to Harlem, Jake," he thought he heard her say as he stepped off the train at Seventh and Lenox Avenues. He wasn't really sure, because his attention was riveted by the sights and sounds bursting from the street. Like the train rumbling the platform, Jake felt a vibration inside that blocked out everything else. It was the pulse of Harlem, the heart of the African-American world— and his new home.

> Hip hip, the joint is jumpin',
> It's really jumpin';
> Come in cats and shake
>   your hats,
> I mean this joint is jumpin'!
> — *Fats Waller*

Harlem is a large neighborhood within New York City. In the 1930s, almost thirty-five thousand blacks lived in its five square miles. Its residents included more African-American scholars, artists, writers, musicians, and business leaders than anywhere else in the world. To Jake it was not just another city. It seemed like another planet.

Jake's mother lived in an apartment building with many other families. Like most structures in Harlem, the building was several stories high. After living in one and two-story houses in Philadelphia with only one family, Jake gasped at the towering building. It seemed there was an entire neighborhood packed within its walls.

The Apartment, 1943

Jake was especially fascinated by the fire escapes. The iron ladders that zig-zagged up the outside of each building were meant for emergency escapes. But more often, they served as tiny porches where tenants stood outside and visited with one another. On muggy summer nights, people often slept on them to escape not fires, but the stifling heat in their apartments. The fire escapes reminded Jake of the biblical story of another Jacob, a shepherd who dreamed of a ladder that stretched to heaven. The iron stairs seemed to reach up and grab the edge of the Harlem sky.

Jake's apartment was tiny compared to his family's Philadelphia home. "This is all I can afford," his mother said sadly. To cheer things up, she covered the floors and walls with brightly colored throw rugs. Jake delighted in the patterns that splashed around the rooms.

Outside, life seemed just as jammed together. Unlike Philadelphia, Harlem had no open fields. The neighborhood boys played stickball in the streets. Stickball was Harlem's version of baseball. Any ball would do, and a stick was used for a bat. Sewer covers, fire hydrants, and other items served as bases. A game would briefly stop when a car passed through the playing "field."

Jake was too shy to join the other boys. He wasn't very good at sports. His favorite pastime was exploring the bustling streets. Each window and doorway he passed told a different story. Some windows framed smoky rooms with men hunched over pool tables. Others showed mothers preparing dinners, or mourners gathered in a funeral parlor.

At night, some windows seemed to burst with the light and laughter of parties. If there was a piano, a musician would be pounding jazz music from its keys. Sometimes even the great Fats Waller dropped in, rolling his eyes as he rocked his three hundred pounds across the piano bench.

There were also tremendous shows in Harlem's entertainment halls. Some, like the Cotton Club, were expensive and open only to white people who traveled to Harlem from other parts of New York City. This seemed strange to Jake, since the performers, including famous musicians like Duke Ellington and Cab Calloway, were all African-American.

But at vaudeville theaters such as the Apollo, black people entertained black audiences. Bill "Bojangles" Robinson tap-danced faster than most people could think. Comedians such as Moms Mabley and Pigmeat Markham made crowds laugh until tears streamed down their faces.

Most theaters also featured a special performance each week called Amateur Night. On Amateur Night, anyone could perform. If the audience was pleased, the hopeful entertainer was invited back and might even be paid next time. If the crowd booed or people held their thumbs down, a giant hook tugged the unfortunate performer off the stage. Even poor families such as Jake's could afford to attend Amateur Night. Several future stars, such as jazz singer Ella Fitzgerald, got their start at Amateur Night.

On Sundays, gatherings of a different type took place. The Abyssinian Baptist Church was the largest Protestant church in the United States. Each week, hundreds

17

Vaudeville, **No. 8 from the** *Theater* **series, 1951**

of Harlem residents crowded in to hear thunderous sermons from Reverend Adam Clayton Powell. Jake's favorite was "The Valley of the Dry Bones." It was a biblical tale of a man whose faith was so strong that he preached to a field of skeletons and brought them back to life. Harlem kids even skipped down the street singing about it:

> The heel bone's connected to the (clap) ankle bone;
> The ankle bone's connected to the (clap) leg bone;
> The leg bone's connected to the (clap) knee bone;
> O hear the word of the Lord!

Harlem's streets also buzzed with the stormy words of "soapbox" lecturers who stood on street corners, often on a ladder or a wooden crate. The speakers shouted to anyone who would listen to their messages. Some were followers of Marcus Garvey, leader of a "Back to Africa" movement. Garveyites encouraged black people to return to Africa, where their ancestors had lived before they were captured and enslaved. They challenged crowds with cries of, "Up, you mighty race!"

Jake decided that Harlem was more fun than frightening. It was a place where black people were not only safe, but respected. African-Americans probably enjoyed more control in Harlem than they did anywhere else. Still, Jake felt that people outside of Harlem dominated his life. This was especially true at school, where he struggled as a student. Compared to the energy outside, Jake's classes seemed as lifeless as the school's name—Public School Number 68. Everyone the students studied in history, science, and other subjects was white—just like the teachers. George Washington was called a great American freedom fighter and hero, though he owned black slaves. To Jake, it felt as if African-Americans had no leaders at all.

"What important things did *our* people do?" Jake wondered. At Public School Number 68, he wasn't getting any answers.

No. 58 from *The Migration of the Negro* series, 1940–41

Chapter 3 PAINTING AND STRUGGLING

Jake's mother sensed his frustration with school, and it worried her. She often worked long hours cleaning buildings, so she could not spend much time with Jake after school. She was afraid her thirteen-year-old son would be recruited by a Harlem gang.

One day Jake's mother brought him to a store-front with a sign that read, "Utopia Children's House." There, she enrolled him in an after-school program. "There's plenty to do, and it will keep you off the streets," she explained.

Jake hesitated; but as usual, he obeyed his mother. A friendly worker introduced himself. "I'm Charles Alston," the young man said with a smile. He explained to Jake that he helped kids with art projects. Jake spotted a bucket of crayons. "Can I color?" he asked.

For months after that, Jake rushed from school to the Utopia Children's House to draw and paint. He advanced from simple patterns on paper to "rooms" made from cardboard boxes and painted with scenes from his apartment, church, barber shops, vaudeville shows—almost everything he saw in Harlem.

The center offered tempera paints because they were the least expensive, but Jake loved their rich, solid colors. He organized his work like a color-by-number

I been scared and battered.
My hopes the wind done scattered.
    Snow has friz me,
    Sun has baked me,
Looks like between 'em they done
    Tried to make me
Stop laughin', stop lovin', stop livin'—
    But I don't care!
    I'm still here!
— *Langston Hughes*

Brooklyn Stoop, 1967

painting. First he painted all the areas he wanted to be a specific color, such as red. Then he might paint all the areas he wanted blue, then yellow, and so on until the painting was complete. Jake tried his hand at making papier-mâché masks, printing from wood blocks he carved—any new form of art he could. But his best work seemed to come when he was painting on paper, cardboard, or whatever material was available.

Charles Alston was becoming recognized as a very good artist himself, but he praised Jake's talents to anyone who would listen. "I don't teach Jake Lawrence; he teaches himself," Alston told others. "The best I can do is help him to find his own way." Still, Jake admired him so much that when Alston got a new job at the Harlem Art Workshop, his star pupil quickly followed.

Besides meeting Alston, another very important thing happened to Jake while he was at the Utopia Children's Center. One day, a visitor named Mr. Allen came to talk about a great hero. To Jake's surprise, it was not one of the usual white heroes, such as George Washington, he heard about in school. The subject was Toussaint L'Ouverture, a black slave on the Caribbean island of Haiti. Toussaint led a slave revolt that created the first black republic in the Western Hemisphere.

Jake's heart pounded, almost as though Toussaint's horse were galloping to battle inside him. Here was a genuine *black* hero. After the talk, he eagerly asked Mr. Allen where he could learn more.

"Go to Professor Seyfert's meetings," the man replied. "The professor gives talks at the YMCA, the 135th Street Library, or any place people will listen."

Jake quickly learned that the "professor" was not a college-trained scholar. He was an African-American carpenter who spent most of his time reading and talking to people about black history. Soon, others in Harlem became interested in his stories about the accomplishments of black people. Like Reverend Powell's sermons, Professor Seyfert's talks rang with excitement.

General Toussaint L'Ouverture, No. 2 from the *Toussaint L'Ouverture* series, 1986

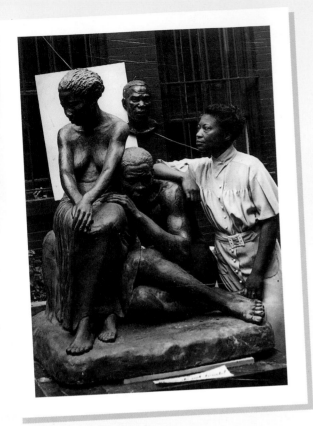

Photo of Augusta Savage, 1936

From Professor Seyfert, Jake learned about Harriet Tubman, a runaway slave who risked her life by returning to the South dozens of times to help other slaves escape. Tubman and her followers traveled at night, using the North Star as their guide. By day, the slaves hid in secret houses along a route that became known as the Underground Railroad. Angry plantation owners offered a reward of $40,000—which would be more than one million dollars today—for her head, but Tubman was never caught. She led more than three hundred slaves to freedom.

Seyfert also talked about Frederick Douglass, a former slave who educated himself and in 1847 founded the first African-American newspaper. Douglass provided the strongest African-American voice against slavery before the Civil War, and so his life was constantly in danger. Jake felt proud of black heroes such as Toussaint, Tubman, and Douglass, who had struggled against the odds and won. He was also angry that they were never mentioned by his teachers at school.

Jake soon relied completely on the people of Harlem for his education. Through Harlem gatherings he met many of the community's best-known writers and artists. Augusta Savage, an artist who had risen from a laundry worker to a sculptor known as far away as Paris, especially encouraged his talents. By the time Jake was sixteen, he knew that he, too, wanted to be an artist. And he decided that he would paint not just what he saw from day to day, but some of the great black heroes whose pictures were rarely in history books.

Unfortunately, as Jake's mother pointed out, art didn't pay the rent or put food on the table. It was the Great Depression—a time when more Americans were out of work than ever before. Soon Jake's mother could not find any work at all. Jake scrambled across Harlem to help make ends meet. He delivered newspapers and laundry, worked in a print shop, even scoured the streets for old bottles that he could sell for a few pennies. Over his mother's objections, Jake quit school so he could help support his family.

Still, he kept painting. Jake attended free evening art classes whenever he could. He met many other young art students, including a smart, pretty girl named Gwendolyn Knight. Gwen was different from many of the other girls Jake knew. She was four years older than he, and she had been born outside the United States, on the Caribbean island of Barbados. Gwen had even attended college, until she ran out of money and had to quit. To Jake's surprise, Gwen took an interest in the shy but very talented boy from Harlem. They soon became close friends.

Jake's work and painting left him little free time. But sometimes he walked more than sixty blocks to the Metropolitan Museum of Art, home of one of the largest art collections in the world. Jake marveled at the works he saw there. He especially liked paintings that told stories. Among his favorites were powerful scenes of struggles painted by Mexican artists such as Diego Rivera

Photo of Jake and Gwen, 1946

25

and José Orozco. Jake liked their simple, dramatic style, and the way that they treated the laborers in their paintings with dignity.

Jake's mother did not share his passion for art. She urged him to go back to school, so he could get what she considered a good job. Though many of the best paying jobs in Harlem went to white people from outside the community, the post office and some city departments were beginning to offer work to educated blacks. "You'll never amount to anything as an artist," she told Jake.

His mother's words burned Jake like the sizzling summer pavement of Harlem's sidewalks. He felt he was learning more than ever. Jake spent hours at the library and other places studying black history. How could all his teachers and friends, even the great Augusta Savage, be wrong about his talent? Jake ignored his mother's warning and centered his world around art.

Jake's paintings were soon highly praised in the community. And his work was displayed in places such as the Harlem YMCA and the library. But these shows didn't bring in any money. Augusta Savage tried to enroll him in a paid program for young artists sponsored by the United States government. "You're too young," Jake was told. "You can't qualify for the program until you're twenty-one years old."

So Jake took a job in another government program, one that accepted younger workers, building a dam in the nearby state of New Jersey. It was the first time Jake had ventured outside New York since his mother moved him there as a child.

The work left him no time to paint, but Jake enjoyed the change. He liked the feeling of the shovel in his hands and the way dirt flew over his shoulders as he dug trenches. He felt powerful, like the workers in the Mexican paintings he admired. Best of all, he was making much more money than he had ever earned before.

"Maybe my mother is right," he sighed as he returned to Harlem when the project ended. "Perhaps I wasn't meant to be an artist."

The Library, 1978

The Studio   H/C   Jacob Lawrence — 1996

Chapter 4 OVERNIGHT SENSATION

"Happy Birthday, Jake." Jake hadn't thought anyone would remember his birthday, but there stood Augusta Savage at his door. She even remembered his age.

"You're twenty-one," Savage noted. "Now you can get into that government art program. Come on." Nobody argued with Augusta Savage, so off they went.

Jake had almost given up hope of making a living as an artist. But for the next eighteen months, he worked on what was called the Easel Project, a program created to provide work for many poor artists across the United States. Jake received his art materials free, and was paid $23.86 per week—more money than many jobs paid during the Depression. All he had to do was give the project two new paintings every six weeks.

Jake felt like the Jacob in the Bible, who had found the ladder to heaven. He was thankful for the chance, and once again he threw himself into painting. Even other young artists marveled at how hard he worked. One of them, a young man named Romare Bearden, almost always finished before Jake did.

"Hey Jake, time for a break," Bearden would suggest. "Let's go shoot some pool."

But Jake remembered the words of one of his childhood instructors: "Good

> You won't get lost in the wilderness
> (Let my people go)
> With a lighted candle at your breast
> (Let my people go)
> Go down, Moses,
>   way down in Egypt land
> Tell old Pharoah, let my people go
>   — *Traditional spiritual*

painters aren't flighty. Painting is hard work. You have to keep at it." And even after everyone else left for the day, Jake kept on painting.

While the Easel Project allowed artists to keep painting, nobody knew what to do with the thousands of works the artists created. Many paintings, including the paintings Jake turned over to the project, vanished. Some were sold to a local plumber. He was not interested in the paintings themselves, but in the canvas used as a painting surface. He ripped the canvases from their frames, and used them to wrap leaky pipes! Because Jake's paintings were created on paper or cardboard surfaces, instead of canvas, they were not used to patch plumbing. Still, nobody knows what happened to his Easel Project paintings. Fortunately, Jake worked so hard that he was able to complete more paintings than those he had given to the Project.

In his spare time, Jake wanted to create a tribute to Touissaint L'Ouverture, the first black hero he had learned about. The problem was, Jake could not decide which part of Toussaint's story to illustrate; his life seemed too big for one picture.

"I want to do a series of paintings that will tell the whole story," Jake told his friend Gwen Knight. To her amazement, he developed ideas for forty-one different paintings. To make matters even more challenging, Jake wanted to create the forty-one paintings using his technique of painting one color at a time. It was not the way most people painted. But Jake felt that the better the colors matched, the more the paintings would work together in telling Toussaint's story.

Gwen helped Jake as he laid forty-one eleven-by-nineteen-inch papers over his entire studio. Then, color by color, Jake worked until all the paintings were finished. His tempera paint dried quickly; so unlike oil paint, which dries slowly, an image could not be changed by painting over it. Jake had to get everything in all the paintings right the first time. Then he wrote a short description of what was happening in each painting. When he was finished, Toussaint's story was told in both pictures and in words.

30

St. Marc, No. 22 from the *Toussaint L'Ouverture* series, 1937–38

Forward Together,
No. 10 from the *Harriet and the Promised Land* series, 1967

People considered the Toussaint series something special, and his supporters helped get it shown in museums in Chicago and Baltimore. This was the first time Jake's work had appeared outside Harlem. He was thrilled, and he soon honored two of his other favorite black heroes, Harriet Tubman and Frederick Douglass, with their own series of paintings.

The new paintings were also popular, especially among African-Americans. Jake was praised not only for his talent but also for giving black people a sense of dignity and pride in their achievements. Jake was only in his early twenties, but like Harriet Tubman's North Star, he was already shining as bright as any black artist before him.

African-American leaders now hoped that Jake's star would shoot across the "white" art world. They wanted to show the world that the works of black people were not "primitive" but just as sophisticated as those by white artists. But Jake was not as bothered by this as some others were. After years of struggle, he was just happy to be painting.

When the Easel Project ended, a grant from a foundation that supported the work of black artists allowed Jake to continue painting. This time, he chose a subject that touched his life even more than the others had: the great African-American migration from the South to the North. Jake had seen some images of the biblical story of Moses and felt that the search by modern-day African-Americans for their own "promised land"—with heroes like Harriet Tubman and the Underground Railroad—was just as dramatic.

With Gwen at his side, Jake worked until his *Migration of the Negro* series was finished. Then, in 1941, they celebrated by getting married. Jake and Gwen took a three-month trip to New Orleans. It was Jake's first trip to the South, and he stayed for a few months to paint what he saw.

Photo of Jacob Lawrence and other Downtown Gallery artists, 1952

While Jake was gone, his *Migration* series was shown to Edith Halpert, one of the world's best-known art gallery owners. She sold paintings by some of America's most famous artists. Unlike some people, Edith Halpert felt that black artists could produce outstanding work. And she had been looking for a talented African-American artist for her Downtown Gallery. She saw Jake's work and knew he was the right one.

This was the first time a major art gallery had shown an African-American's work. Jake soon learned how much this meant. Not just one, but *two* of the nation's finest art museums wanted to purchase the entire *Migration* series. The sixty paintings were divided between New York's Museum of Modern Art and The Phillips Collection in Washington, D.C.

At about the same time, *Fortune,* one of the nation's largest magazines, used twenty-six of the *Migration* paintings in a special section on blacks in America. Complimentary letters poured in to the magazine. To many people, black and white, Jake's paintings symbolized the search for a better life by people of all races throughout history. The events depicted in the *Migration* series were compared to the flight of Jewish people from the ruthless German dictator Adolf Hitler, which was taking place in Europe at that time.

A month after Jake's paintings appeared in *Fortune,* the United States declared war on Germany. Jake joined the U.S. Navy to fight in World War II. Like many African-Americans in the armed forces, he was assigned to cleaning the eating and

No. 3 from the *Migration of the Negro* series, 1940–41

living quarters of white officers. In the building where the men were housed, blacks were separated from whites.

Within a few months, Jake had sunk from being a respected artist to a mistreated sailor. Fortunately, he soon received a much better assignment. Carlton Skinner, the commander of the patrol vessel on which Jake was stationed, made a proposal that was then unheard of in the Navy. He wanted his ship to be completely integrated. This meant that white sailors would not automatically get better jobs than blacks. And members of both races would have equal chances for advancement, based on their skills, not their color.

Commander Skinner saw Jake's artwork and immediately added painting to his official duties. For the rest of the war, Jake painted the men at their jobs on the ship. Unlike many other military artists, he didn't focus on sailors in moments of actual fighting; Jake concentrated on everyday events.

"It's the little things that are big," Jake explained. "A man may never see combat, but he can be a very important person. The man at the guns, there's glamour there. But the cook—the cooks may not like my style of painting, but they appreciate the fact that I'm painting a cook."

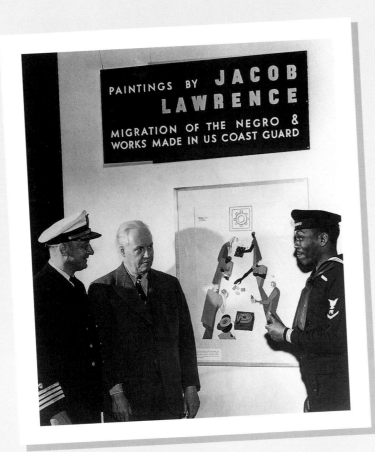

Jacob with one of his Coast Guard paintings at an exhibition opening at the Museum of Modern Art, 1944

Photo of Jacob speaking to students about his *Toussaint L'Ouverture* series, 1941

When the war ended, Jake left the military. During the 1940s he created more than two hundred fifty paintings and they were always among the most popular at Edith Halpert's Downtown Gallery. *Time* magazine proclaimed that, at age thirty, Jacob Lawrence was the nation's number one black artist.

Jake began to feel uneasy about such tributes. People discussed his work as black art, as if it were something separate from art. Some even connected his work to African art. Jake had never even been to Africa, and he was just as influenced by Mexican muralists and seventeenth century Dutch masters as he was by African art. He wanted to be considered a great artist, period.

Jake was also bothered that no other African-American artists, including his friends and former teachers, were as acclaimed by the art world. He began to feel guilty. Why had he already soared to greater popularity than other talented black artists? He began to wonder if he deserved it.

Despite his fame, Jake began to feel isolated from other artists, both white and black. After beginning the 1940s by zooming to the top of the art world, by the end of the decade the pressure brought everything crashing down on him. He felt out of control and entered a hospital for help. This was hardly what he expected when he decided to become an artist.

Chapter 5

BLACK AND WHITE

Jake stayed in the hospital for nine months. He found a doctor who helped him realize that nothing was wrong with him; his rapid fame had simply brought challenges he had not expected. With the doctor's help, Jake learned how to handle the pressures of being famous and regained his confidence.

Even in the hospital, Jake couldn't resist his creative urges. He set up a small studio in his room and painted the people around him. He showed them gardening, taking medication, and wandering aimlessly through the halls. Unlike Jake, many of the patients had serious mental problems. Some would never leave the hospital. With his usual honesty, Jake revealed their sad, restless feelings. "These people are facing a struggle inside themselves that is just as intense as that of the freedom fighters I've painted," he noted.

> I have a dream that my four little children will one day live in a nation where they will not be judged by the color of their skin but by the content of their character.
> — *Martin Luther King, Jr.*

Jake's paintings broke new ground. It was the first time a popular artist had looked closely at the lives of emotionally disturbed people. Critics finally began regarding him less as a black artist, and more as simply a great artist. Now, Jake felt surer of himself than ever.

Over the next several years, Jake painted a wide variety of subjects. He still created an occasional series, such as *Struggle: From the History of the American*

Depression, 1950

39

People, which portrayed thirty scenes from early American history. Other work sprang from his increasingly wide travels, including trips to Africa. There, he found that the brightly colored villages and bustling marketplaces were perfect subjects for his style of painting.

But wherever Jake roamed, he always returned to his home—New York. And he continued to turn to Harlem for subjects. Some scenes painted during this time were as lively as those he painted a generation earlier, but others pointed out the sad decay in his boyhood home. The Harlem Renaissance had ended, and the community was facing increasing poverty and crime. Jake, as always, painted what he saw. *Slums*, for example, showed run-down apartment buildings viewed from a window swarming with cockroaches.

By now, African-Americans across the United States were becoming increasingly frustrated. Almost one hundred years after slavery had ended, most blacks were still much poorer than whites. Jake had become one of the most respected artists in the world, but in some American cities he was not allowed in hotels, restaurants, even public restrooms. A new generation of African-American leaders, such as the Reverend Martin Luther King Jr., demanded an end to such segregation. They organized large protests against places that excluded blacks—from buses to schools to businesses.

Jake turned his attention to this new American struggle. While some whites supported and even joined the black "freedom marchers," others reacted violently to these efforts. Many of the paintings Jake created during the 1960s showed African-Americans being attacked as they marched in a rally or tried to enter an all-white facility. "Some people may hate me for holding up a mirror," he said, "but I can't drop it."

Confrontation at the Bridge, 1975

Time magazine cover of Jesse Jackson, 1970

Jake created a portrait of African-American leader Reverend Jesse Jackson for the cover of *Time* magazine, and he lent his talents to civil rights causes. He even breathed new life into some black heroes he had painted in the past, such as Harriet Tubman. Jake illustrated a children's book called *Harriet and the Promised Land*, because he felt that young people, especially African-Americans, could be inspired by the struggles of this brave woman.

Jake painted Harriet large—as she was in life—and emphasized what he considered her strong features, such as her hands and feet. When a librarian complained that the paintings made her look "grotesque and ugly," Jake replied that "Harriet Tubman wasn't on a Sunday School picnic. She was in a struggle for people's lives, which is a beautiful thing. Ugly is how someone acts, not how they look."

To Jake's surprise, the most frequent complaints against him in these days came from some of the same African-Americans whose struggles he supported. They argued that if Jake truly cared for his race, he would lend his voice as well as his paintings to civil rights. If he really supported African-American artists, they said, he would reject the white people who had long dominated the art world. They felt that Jake should support only black artists, and lead an all-black art movement.

No. 15 from the *Harriet and the Promised Land* series, 1967

"Some artists are crusaders; I'm not," Jake tried to explain. Jake preferred to speak with pictures, not words. Besides, he did not want to condemn every white person. Whites such as Edith Halpert and Commander Skinner had helped him along the way, just as the Harlem community had. To Jake, the issues weren't as "black and white" as the races of people. Jake felt that art should be appreciated for the colors of the paintings, not the color of the artist's skin. For years, he had worked to be accepted as an artist, regardless of race. His success had opened the door for other African-American artists, including his old friend from the Easel Project, Romare Bearden. And he had introduced audiences of all races to black heroes such as Harriet Tubman.

Many young African-Americans were not aware of the struggles of previous generations. Some called Jake an "Uncle Tom." This was an insult used to describe black people who adopted white people's ways to get their approval. Jake had never adopted anyone's ways or artistic styles but his own. But by now, he had learned not to be bothered by such remarks. "Young people should be aggressive and question the way things are," Jake said. "Harriet Tubman, in her day, would have been considered a radical."

Still, it seemed there were days when he could not please anyone. As a guest teacher at a New York art school, he never knew where to sit in the cafeteria. All the black students sat together, but he never seemed welcome in their group. He was not considered "one of them." Yet, he was criticized if he sat somewhere else.

"I just can't win," Jake shrugged. Though he had learned not to get too upset by the problems created by his fame and beliefs, Jake was ready for a change.

People in Other Rooms, 1975

Chapter 6

BUILDING BROTHERHOOD

Jake may have felt uncomfortable in college cafeterias, but he was right at home in the classroom. He had been a guest instructor at many schools for more than twenty years, and he was constantly in demand. Jake enjoyed sharing ideas with students and encouraging their talents. And he never forgot the art teachers in Harlem who had helped him succeed.

Even though Jake was now one of the most admired artists in the world, he didn't try to dictate how others should paint. "He guides you without dominating you," one of his students said. But he made sure nobody gave less than their best effort. Once a student turned in a painting that was not well organized. He told Jake that the jumbled appearance was his "style"; that was how he wanted it to look. "Don't bluff," Jake frowned. "If you paint, do it well or not at all."

One of Jake's short-term teaching jobs was at the University of Washington in Seattle. A year later, in 1971, he was invited to become a full-time professor. For a lifelong New Yorker, it was a big decision. Seattle was on the opposite coast of the United States, almost three thousand miles away from New York. It was a nice place to visit, but did he and Gwen really want to live there?

They decided to give it a try, and they have never moved back. It seemed to be exactly the change Jake needed. He taught at the University of Washington

> Let us learn together and laugh together and pray together, confident that in the end we will triumph together in the right.
> — *Jimmy Carter*

Carpenters, 1977

47

Photo of Jacob teaching at the University of Washington, 1984

for the next twelve years. Even after Jake retired, the Lawrences continued to call Seattle home.

Like New York, Seattle is a melting pot of races and cultures. But the mix is a bit different. Since Seattle borders the Pacific Ocean, it attracts many immigrants from Asian nations, such as China and Japan. It is also the home of many Native Americans, whose ancestors lived in the northwestern United States before European settlers arrived. Despite their differences, the groups get along fairly well.

In the 1970s, Seattle was a rapidly growing city. Jake loved to watch the construction that seemed to be springing up everywhere. It reminded him of his Harlem boyhood. He looked at a hammer and thought about how the same type of tool was used to create buildings in the days of Harriet Tubman, and even in the ancient times of Moses.

Jake began to collect tools, and as he looked over his collection, he considered what "building" meant to him. It stood for creating not just structures but better lives. "Some of my paintings show man's struggle, but building shows the beauty of people working together," he said.

Many of the paintings that Jake created during this time contain a building theme. He filled the scenes with his own hand tools, and included workers of many colors. Jake often added children and families to suggest that people of all races and ages must work together to build the future. The *Builders* paintings have become some of his most popular works.

48

The Builders, 1974

Olympische Spiele München 1972

In Seattle, Jake's imagination soared like the mountains that surround the city. With the help of assistants, he produced large murals for colleges, city buildings, and even the Kingdome sports stadium. Soon he was asked to create murals in other cities, such as New York and Washington, D.C. Like the Mexican muralists he admired in his youth, he was now documenting his nation's people on its walls.

Sometimes he was hired to paint his own view of a special event, such as the Olympic Games. Jake liked the Olympics for two reasons. First, he loved to portray the movement of muscular athletes. And much like his *Builders* subjects, Olympic athletes met in a spirit of cooperation. Jake's paintings were often made into posters seen throughout the world.

Jake also expanded his style as he took on new and different subjects. He illustrated an edition of *Aesop's Fables* with twenty-three pen-and-ink drawings. It was the first series Jake had ever created that featured animals instead of people. First he drew the figures in the pictures as people, then finished them with animal faces and bodies.

In 1977, Jake was one of five famous American artists invited to the swearing in ceremony for President Jimmy Carter. Other artists focused on the president, but Jake took a different view. Instead of looking forward to the speaker's podium, he gazed back at the crowds. Despite the bitterly cold day, every chair and standing space was occupied. People even scrambled up trees to see the new president.

To Jake, it was truly the "People's Inauguration" that President Carter had wanted. His painting *The Swearing In* featured everyday people who braved the weather to welcome their new leader. They cheered and waved American flags, and they clapped through their thick gloves. It became one of President Carter's favorite images.

By now, Jake was sixty years old, but his popularity was continuing to grow. An American art school wanted to donate a painting to the Catholic Church's Vatican Museum in Italy, one of the world's finest art collections. The Pope was given a choice of a work by any American artist. He chose one of Jake's *Builders* paintings.

After more than five decades as a world-famous painter, the modest artist has been honored by leaders of many nations. Whether it is a single image of a room in Harlem or a series showing a migration across the United States, Jacob Lawrence's work contains stories for everyone.

The Swearing In, 1977

BIBLIOGRAPHY

Aesop's Fables, illustrated by Jacob Lawrence (Seattle, WA: University of Washington Press, 1997).

Harriet and the Promised Land, illustrated by Jacob Lawrence (New York, NY: Doubleday, 1972).

Jacob Lawrence, by Milton Brown (New York, NY: Whitney Museum of American Art, 1974).

Jacob Lawrence, by Aline Saarinen (New York, NY: American Federation of Arts, 1960).

Jacob Lawrence, American Painter, by Ellen Harkins Wheat (Seattle, WA: University of Washington Press, 1986).

Jacob Lawrence: The Migration Series, by Elizabeth Hutton Turner (Washington, D.C.: The Rappahannock Press, 1993).

Jacob Lawrence: Thirty Years of Prints, by Peter Nesbett (Seattle, WA: University of Washington Press, 1994).

Six Black Masters of American Art, by Romare Bearden and Harry Henderson (New York, NY: Doubleday, 1972).

CAPTIONS AND CREDITS

All paintings and prints are by Jacob Lawrence. Unless otherwise indicated, artwork is reproduced courtesy of the artist and Francine Seders Gallery, Seattle, Washington. For all dimensions, height precedes width.

page 4: *Self-Portrait*, 1977; gouache on paper, 23 × 31"; National Academy, New York. Photo: Glenn Castellano

page 6: No. 1 from the *Migration of the Negro* series, 1940–41; tempera on Masonite, 12 × 18"; The Phillips Collection, Washington, D.C. Photo: Edward Owen.

page 7: From COLLECTED POEMS by Langston Hughes. Copyright © 1994 by the Estate of Langston Hughes. Reprinted by permission of Alfred A. Knopf Inc.

page 8: Photo: Courtesy of Francine Seders Gallery.

page 9: *The Ant and the Grasshopper*, 1969; ink on paper, 15 × 14½". Photo: Spike Mafford.

page 10: *Tombstones*, 1942; gouache on paper, 28¾ × 20½"; Whitney Museum of American Art, New York. Photo: Geoffrey Clements, © 1998 Whitney Museum of American Art.

page 12: *This Is Harlem*, 1942; No. 1 from the *Harlem* series; gouache on paper, 14½ × 22"; Hirshhorn Museum and Sculpture Garden, Smithsonian Institution, Gift of Joseph H. Hirshhorn, 1966. Photo: Ricardo Blanc.

page 13: Lyrics from *The Joint Is Jumpin'*, by Thomas "Fats" Waller, Andy Razaf and J. C. Johnson © 1938 (Renewed) Razaf Music Co., Record Music Publishing Co. and Chappell & Co. All Rights Reserved. Used by Permission. WARNER BROS. PUBLICATIONS U.S. INC., Miami, FL 33014.

page 14: *The Apartment*, 1943; gouache on paper, 21¼ × 29¼"; Hunter Museum of American Art, Chattanooga, Tennessee, Museum purchase with funds provided by the Benwood Foundation and the 1982 Collectors' Group.

page 16: *Vaudeville*, 1951; No. 8 from the *Theater* series; tempera on fiberboard with pencil, 30 × 20"; Hirshhorn Museum and Sculpture Garden, Smithsonian Institution, Gift of Joseph H. Hirshhorn, 1966. Photo: Lee Stalsworth.

page 19: No. 58 from the *Migration of the Negro* series, 1940–41; tempera on gesso on composition board, 12 × 18"; The Museum of Modern Art, New York, Gift of Mrs. David M. Levy. Photo: © 1998 The Museum of Modern Art.

page 20: *Brooklyn Stoop*, 1967; gouache and casein on paper, 21¼ × 16¼"; Tacoma Art Museum, Tacoma, WA.

page 21: From COLLECTED POEMS by Langston Hughes. Copyright © 1994 by the Estate of Langston Hughes. Reprinted by permission of Alfred A. Knopf Inc.

page 23: *General Toussaint L'Ouverture*, 1986; screenprint after No. 2 of the *Toussaint L'Ouverture* series, 1937–38; 32¼ × 22". Photo: Spike Mafford.

page 24: Photo: Photographs and Prints Division, Schomburg Center for Research in Black Culture, The New York Public Library, Astor, Lenox and Tilden Foundations.

pages 26–27: *The Library*, 1978; screenprint, 10¼ × 15¼". Photo: Spike Mafford.

page 28: *The Studio*, 1996; lithograph, 30 × 22". Photo: Spike Mafford.

page 31: *St. Marc*, 1994; screenprint after No. 22 of the *Toussaint L'Ouverture* series, 1937–38; 32¼ × 22¼". Photo: Spike Mafford.

page 32: *Forward Together*, 1997; screenprint after *Forward*, No. 10 from the *Harriet and the Promised Land* series, 1967; 25½ × 40". Photo: Richard Nicol.

page 34: Photo: © 1998 Louis Faurer.

page 35: No. 3 from the *Migration of the Negro* series, 1940–41; tempera on Masonite, 12 × 18". Photo: Edward Owen, © The Phillips Collection, Washington, D.C.

page 36: Photo: Photographs and Prints Division, Schomburg Center for Research in Black Culture, The New York Public Library, Astor, Lenox and Tilden Foundations.

page 37: Photo: Courtesy of The George Arents Research Library, Syracuse University.

page 38: *Depression*, 1950; tempera on paper, 22 × 30½"; Whitney Museum of American Art, New York, Gift of David M. Solinger. Photo: Geoffrey Clements, © 1997 Whitney Museum of American Art.

page 41: *Confrontation at the Bridge*, 1975; screenprint, 19½ × 26". Photo: Spike Mafford.

page 42: *Time* magazine cover, April 6, 1970; reproduction of *Jesse Jackson*, 1970; © 1970 TIME Inc. Reprinted by permission.

page 43: No. 15 from the *Harriet and the Promised Land* series, 1967; gouache on paper; Private collection. Photo: Spike Mafford, courtesy Francine Seders Gallery, Seattle.

page 45: *People in Other Rooms*, 1975; screenprint, 30½ × 22¼". Photo: Paul Macapia.

page 46: *Carpenters*, 1977; lithograph, 21¾ × 25¾". Photo: Spike Mafford.

page 48: Photo: © 1998 Chris Eden.

page 49: *The Builders*, 1974; screenprint, 34 × 25¾". Photo: Spike Mafford.

page 50: *Olympic Games*, 1971; screenprint, 42½ × 27½". Photo: Spike Mafford.

pages 52–53: *The Swearing In*, 1977; screenprint, 20 × 30". Photo: Spike Mafford.

page 57: *Bread, Fish, Fruit*, 1985. Photo: Chris Eden.

© 1998 by John Duggleby.
All rights reserved.

Book design and illustration by John Hubbard.
Typeset in Geometric415, with display type in
Daddy-O-Square.
Produced by Marquand Books, Inc., Seattle.
Printed in China.

Library of Congress Cataloging-in-Publication Data
Duggleby, John.
    Story painter : the life of Jacob Lawrence / by John
Duggleby.
      p.   cm.
    Includes bibliographical references.
    Summary: A biography of the African American artist
who grew up in the midst of the Harlem Renaissance
and became one of the most renowned painters of the
life of his people.
    ISBN 0-8118-2082-3 (hc)
    1. Lawrence, Jacob, 1917–   —Juvenile literature.
2. Afro-American painters—Biography. 3. Afro-
Americans in art—Juvenile literature. [1. Lawrence,
Jacob, 1917– . 2. Artists. 3. Afro-Americans in art.
 4. Afro-Americans—Biography. 5. Art appreciation.]
I. Lawrence, Jacob. II. Title.
ND237.L29D83 1998
759.13—dc21
[B]   98-4513
                      CIP
                        AC

Distributed in Canada by Raincoast Books
8680 Cambie Street, Vancouver,
British Columbia V6P 6M9

10 9 8 7 6 5 4 3 2 1

Chronicle Books
85 Second Street, San Francisco, California 94105

www.chroniclebooks.com

Bread, Fish, Fruit, 1985